PETERBOROUGH
IN 100 DATES

JEAN A. HOOPER

1

First published 2015

The History Press
The Mill, Brimscombe Port
Stroud, Gloucestershire, GL5 2QG
www.thehistorypress.co.uk

British Library Cataloguing in Publication Data.
A catalogue record for this book is available from the British Library.

ISBN 978 0 7509 6153 0

Typesetting and origination by The History Press
Printed in Great Britain

Contents

Acknowledgements

Thanks to Mike and Dora who patiently helped me research documents and old newspapers and then read the finished text.

All images are property of The History Press unless otherwise credited.

Introduction

Since the first prehistoric settlements along the Fen Edge, Peterborough has become an independent city authority of nearly 190,000 people. Beginning as a Saxon settlement by the Nene known as Medeshampstead, the community increased in importance when a monastery was established by a member of the Mercian royal family in the middle of the seventh century. As the monastery became richer and more influential it drew trade and wealth to the town and when the Benedictine abbey received charters of rights from successive kings of England, the abbots' power extended over the whole local area. Markets and fairs brought traders from far afield and pilgrims travelled to the abbey of St Peter bringing offerings that made the town even wealthier. The abbey completely dominated life until it was closed by Henry VIII yet its political power had been so absolute that town government was still affected centuries later.

Peterborough became a city in 1541 but was still a small market town where agriculture played a major part in the local economy. Unlike nearby towns such as Stamford, Peterborough did not even have a newspaper. All this changed in the mid-nineteenth century, however, with the coming of the railways. As people moved to the city to work for railway companies, major engineering works were developed and the town began to grow quickly away from the medieval centre. Firms such as Perkins, Peterbrotherhood and Baker Perkins became major employers, as did the brick making industry.

In the late 1960s, Peterborough began another major stage of expansion over a relatively short period of time. In 1967 it was designated as a New Town, which would see townships built around the edges of the centre, dramatically increasing the population. Thousands of houses have been built in Bretton, Orton, Werrington and Hampton as the city continues to attract new companies into an area where the workforce can find accommodation and good transport links. Although some development has occurred in the city centre, for example the Queensgate Shopping Centre, the layout of the main area still shows the pattern of the Middle Ages. The small city centre, the surrounding countryside and rich agricultural land still retain a feeling of what was important in Peterborough's past.

This book looks at events that have marked life in the area from the first days of settlement. Significant changes in the town can often be related to a single incident. National wars, conflict and politics affected the lives of ordinary residents, as did the affairs of important men and women who were associated with the town. Descriptions of social occasions reflect how townspeople enjoyed their leisure time, either as participants or spectators at major celebrations. Peterborough is a growing city of many nationalities, looking to the future, but its character has been created by events in its past.

About the Author

JEAN A. HOOPER has been a Blue Badge Guide for Peterborough for more than twenty years. She is also a cathedral guide and leads tours throughout the year. She lives in Peterborough.

PETERBOROUGH
IN 100 DATES

17 April

According to Bede's *The Ecclesiastical History of the English People*, the founder of the first Christian church in Peterborough (then known as Medeshampstead) was murdered at Easter in AD 656 by his treacherous wife. He was local ruler Peada, son of the King of Mercia, and in about AD 655 he had married a Northumbrian princess. His bride's father insisted that Peada convert to Christianity and four monks accompanied him back to Medeshampstead to establish a small monastery.

Although there is no contemporary account, later kings, including Peada's brother Wulfhere, ensured that Medeshampstead continued to increase in size and importance by gifts of land and privileges. From such small beginnings grew the great abbey, which saw the development of the surrounding area and the subsequent wealth of the town. When a wall was built round the monastery at the end of the tenth century, the town became known as a 'burh', a fortified place. As the abbey was dedicated to Saints Peter, Paul and Andrew, the town became known as the burh of St Peter, then Peterborough.

22 November

Peterborough monk Hugh Candidus wrote the history of the abbey from its foundation, drawing on earlier writings and describing events that had taken place over two centuries earlier. The year AD 870 seems to have been catastrophic for the monastery and town, and Candidus's history describes how Viking raiders set fire to houses and plundered the monastery, killing all but one of the monks there. Candidus's account also refers to the abbot of the time, Hedda, whose name is traditionally linked to the Hedda or Monks' Stone. This important Saxon sculpture is one of the oldest objects in the cathedral. A chronicle reputedly written by Ingulph of Crowland likewise describes the events of this time and gives the date of 22 November as the day of the massacre.

Nevertheless, the dates and exact events remain merely conjecture. In fact, it is difficult to know just what damage was done to the town and monastery by the Danes. Viking raiders plundered the wealth of the eastern part of England every year but by the late ninth century they were beginning to settle here permanently. There is no doubt that the 'Great Army' made its way through East Anglia at this time, asserting its power over the Saxon kingdoms, and it is likely that the monasteries entered a period of decline. Whether or not the monastery was completely destroyed, it is impossible to say with certainty.

2 June

Peterborough saw some of its fiercest fighting in the Battle of Bolhithe Gate in 1070. This date saw the Danish army and their local Saxon ally, Hereward 'the Wake', attack the abbey, intent on plundering its riches before the arrival of Abbot Turold.

Turold, a Norman who had been appointed by William the Conqueror to help quell Saxon resistance, was travelling to Peterborough with his army at the beginning of June when he heard news of the raid. Monks had sent messages asking for the abbot's aid when the Danes crossed the Fens and arrived on the south side of the abbey where the original Saxon town lay. Unfortunately, Abbot Turold and his forces arrived too late to stop the impending attack and those inside the abbey had been left to hide what treasures they could before preparing to defend themselves. At first they managed to hold back the attackers but, as the battle raged, the Danes set fire to the gate and were able to break through into the abbey. The fire destroyed many of the buildings near the gate and burned down most of the town, though the church itself survived. The abbey was robbed of its treasures before the Danes and their allies fled into the Fens.

4 August

Fire was a constant threat to life and property when nearly every building, and certainly ordinary homes, were built mainly of wood and thatch. On this date, and not for the first time in Peterborough's history, a fire destroyed the town and burnt down most of the abbey. The church was severely damaged and the blaze in the tower lasted for nine days, according to the account of an eyewitness, Hugh Candidus. The chapter house, the monks' dormitory and the new refectory, where the monks had eaten for only four days, were the only buildings in the monastery that survived the fire.

Candidus recorded that the abbot, John de Sais, had become so angry on the day of the fire that he left for his house in Castor, cursing the monastery as he went. Later that day, when one of those responsible for the bake house was unable to light a fire, he shouted 'Devil light the fire' and flames shot up and spread right through the monastery and town.

The damage to the Saxon church meant that rebuilding had to begin, this time in the Norman style, resulting in the much bigger cathedral that remains today. The Normans may well have rebuilt the church at some point; the fire gave them the opportunity.

29 June

Abbot Martin de Bec was appointed on St Peter's Day 1133 and was responsible for Peterborough's first 'New Town'. The rebuilding of the abbey was already underway and the new, bigger, Norman church meant that changes had to be made to the area around the monastery. The original small Saxon town or 'vill' was behind the present-day cathedral by the river, an area that often flooded. The small market meant that there was no room to expand trade and increase revenue, so the market place and town centre were moved to the great Western Gate of the monastery. The large marketstede or square remained the market place until 1963 and the streets that grew up around it gave the town its shape. Although people still lived in the old Saxon settlement, the area never really developed as the new town did. Even in Victorian times this area of the city remained poor while the new market brought more trade and wealth to the rest of Peterborough and buildings spread along streets such as Westgate, Cumbergate and Howegate. 'Gate' (*gata*) was the Danish word for a roadway and Howegate, Midgate today, led round past the 'howe' or mound of the former castle. The pattern of Martin le Bec's new town is still evident today.

29 June

The right to hold markets and fairs was a privilege granted by the king and brought wealth and importance to a town. Peterborough had held a market since the tenth century but in 1189 King Richard I granted a charter to Abbot Benedict which allowed him to hold a fair for St Peter's Day on 29 June each year. It was held over two days and was on a larger scale than a normal weekly market.

The main reason for a fair in the twelfth century was for trade. People travelled to Peterborough from some distance, bringing animals and goods for sale or buying merchandise from traders in the town. Money was collected from traders and stallholders, and those who tried to sell poor-quality animals or meat were fined at special courts held on market days to deal with petty crime before offenders left town. Extra income came from those travelling into Peterborough to spend their money in the inns and taverns as well as at the stalls, and the fair provided a chance to have a good time, with travelling entertainers and archery competitions amongst the attractions designed to entertain the crowds. The first of Peterborough's fairs was not the largest but would certainly have boosted the local economy.

6 October

The Bishop of Lincoln, Robert Grosseteste, and the Bishop of Exeter, William Brewer, led the dedication service for the new abbey church of St Peter on this date. Work had begun to rebuild the church on a much greater scale shortly after the Nine Days' Fire and, for 120 years from 1118, life in the abbey would have carried on as the building, which is now the cathedral, took shape.

Barnack stone was brought in barges along the Nene and other waterways, and then taken up to the abbey where the wooden windlass, used to haul these blocks of stone up to the top of the building, is still in place today. The builders kept to the Norman style of architecture for over 100 years, making the completed structure one of the country's major Norman buildings.

Today the cathedral still dominates the city centre but when it was finally completed it would have dwarfed the small town where stone was rarely used for building. At the same time, the charters of the abbey would have confirmed its possessions and rights. The new church served to emphasise the importance and wealth of Peterborough's abbey and its influence on the development of the city.

29 December

On this day, Godfrey of Crowland became abbot and soon began many building projects in and around the abbey. His works included erecting walls, houses and a private garden – the latter in the area of Bishop's Road Gardens. One of the most important of his improvements was the building of a bridge over the river.

The first mention of a bridge over the Nene in Peterborough was in 1308. It was made of wood but was broken up by ice soon after it was built and a new, stronger one was constructed. Where previously people had to cross the Nene by boat or go across the ford slightly to the east, this new bridge gave easier access to Peterborough. At this time, in the centuries before the embankment of the Nene, the area by the ford and the small river port would often flood (especially in winter) making the crossing more challenging. A bridge meant that people and goods could approach the abbey and markets more easily, improving the local economy. Several small waterways surrounded and ran through the town but Hithegate (the road to the port) followed the route from the new bridge to the abbey gates. Bridge Street follows the same route, giving the shape of the town to this day.

15 June

The Black Death reduced England's population dramatically in the fourteenth century, wiping out many of those who worked in the fields for their landlords. In some areas, not enough labourers were left to gather or plant crops and animals were dying through lack of food and care. The feudal system that operated at the time meant that peasants were 'owned' by the Lords of the Manor in which they lived and had few rights of their own. However, as landowners grew desperate for workers, their tenants were able to demand more money and rights in return for their service. After the introduction of a poll tax, which restricted the amount a peasant could earn, rebellion spread throughout the country.

In Peterborough, the tenants of the abbot attacked the abbey and were only stopped from overwhelming the monks by the arrival of the 'Fighting Bishop' of Norwich, Hugh le Despenser. Apparently always ready for a fight, he is said to have worn armour under his robes! Despenser ruthlessly drove his troops into the mob at the abbey gates, even hacking some protestors to death in the Becket Chapel where they sought refuge. He hanged the ringleaders before leaving the town and ended the revolt in Peterborough.

4 July

Philippa, daughter of Henry Bolingbroke, later Henry IV, was born in Peterborough on 4 July 1394. Unfortunately, the birth resulted in the death of her mother, Mary de Bohun, on the same day.

Mary was Henry's first wife and they had six children, including the future Henry V. Two of their children were daughters, named Blanche and Philippa. Following her death, Mary was buried in Leicester even though Peterborough was her 'favourite manor'; she had spent a lot of time in the town and was certainly in residence during 1391–92 when Blanche was born.

Philippa was baptised in Peterborough Abbey, as was her older sister. Some details of Blanche's christening are known and it is likely that the ceremony for Philippa was the same. The font was draped with 3 ells (about 3m) of Flemish linen and 3 ells of Champagne linen. Flemish linen was often used for church cloths whilst linen from the Champagne area of France was known at the time for its quality. The baby's nurse received 6 ells of canvas for use on her bed, which would have been a simple pallet or mattress on the floor. When Henry became king in 1399 both of his daughters were elevated to the rank of princess.

24 June

Peterborough's first parish church was situated in the Boongate area of the city in the original Saxon settlement. When a 'New Town' was created in the twelfth century in front of the abbey's great Western Gate, the market place was moved and gradually people began to live around it. They still worshipped at the old church but getting there in winter was difficult because of flooding. Nearly 300 years passed before a new, more accessible, parish church was built in the centre of the market place. The original church was demolished, as was the nave of St Thomas' Chapel (Becket's Chapel) on the left of the cathedral gates, and the stone was used to build the new parish church of St John the Baptist in the area where butchers' market stalls traditionally stood. For this reason, the site was cleaned first, after years of being contaminated by the blood of slaughtered animals. That is why the church still stands 'in a hole', at a lower level than the square around it. It was dedicated for use on 24 June 1407. Henry IV, formerly Henry Bolingbroke, Earl of Derby, was king at the time and his emblem, an antelope, was placed above the entrance. A new public cemetery was located on the north side of the abbey church.

14 July

In July 1439, King Henry VI gave a charter to the abbot that allowed him to hold a fair on 21 September, St Matthew's Day, every year. The fair lasted for three days and was to be held 'at the bridge of Peterborough by the River Nene'. Money was raised by charging those who wanted to buy and sell but it seems that the abbot sold these rights to the highest bidder, thus guaranteeing a good income. There were prayers in the abbey church before a procession to the fields by the river, where a proclamation was read to declare the fair open and to call upon everyone to 'behave in a sober fashion'. As with Peterborough's other fairs – St Peter's Fair, Ram Fair and Cherry Fair – trade was the reason for its existence, though there were plenty of things to keep the visitors amused. The many drinking booths meant fighting was common and punishments were swiftly meted out. Over time, as shops developed to provide goods all year round, trade decreased and leisure pursuits increased. Bridge Fair is now a funfair but is still proclaimed open by the mayor and a sausage supper marks the occasion.

20 January

Peterborough's location, near the major routes north and south, east and west, meant that, at times of troop movements, armies often passed through or close by the town. In 1461, during the Wars of the Roses, the dangers of this were highlighted when – following the Battle of Wakefield, where Richard of York and his son were killed – Lancastrian soldiers began moving south.

The troops took food and supplies from town and countryside as they went, spreading great fear amongst the local population. The chronicler of Crowland Abbey reported that the monks set up what defences they could, putting stakes and fences at places where the soldiers could get across the water to attack. The Abbot of Ely, meanwhile, hired mercenaries from Burgundy to protect his abbey, but whether Peterborough took any precautions or not, the town was plundered as the Lancastrians passed through in January.

Fotheringhay Castle was associated with the House of York and Richard III was born there in 1452. As Duke of Gloucester, Richard led the great funeral procession to Fotheringhay for the reburial of his father and older brother fifteen years after their death at the Battle of Wakefield. Their reburial in the family vault was attended by thousands of people including King Edward IV; they attended a feast in the castle and pavilions that had been set up for the occasion.

13 March

After Robert Kirkton became abbot in March 1497, he completed major alterations to the abbey church. The construction of the 'New Building' extended the length of the church in a new style of architecture. The most noticeable difference is the fan-vaulted ceiling, probably the work of John Wastell, who went on to design the ceiling of King's College Chapel in Cambridge.

Kirkton was not popular with the monks and often came into conflict with the townspeople. Angry mobs gathered outside the abbey when tempers boiled over during several disputes but matters came to a head in 1517. His construction of a deer park caused the demolition of several houses in the Boongate area and also took some of the public burial ground. Furthermore, he tried to stop the townspeople using common land at Flag Fen so that he could use it for his own animals. Forty men decided to take the law into their own hands and armed themselves against attack before cutting the hay on the Fen for their own use and taking it away. The dispute went before the Star Chamber, which decided cases involving those too important to be dealt with by local courts. The result of this quarrel is not known but Kirkton's influence on the architecture of the abbey can be seen in the cathedral today.

1 August

In 1502 Sir William Fitzwilliam paid 1,200 marks (about £800) to Robert Whittlebury for 'The manors of Milton Marham with their appurtenances in Milton, Marham, Caster, Etton, Maxsey, Norborough and Depyngate ... and the wharfage and the profits of the wharf and water of Gunwade' (now known as Milton Ferry). The deeds were handed over in front of the font in St Paul's Cathedral in London as a sign of honesty and good faith in the transaction. Thus began the area's association with the Fitzwilliam family, which has had such a major impact on the life of the city and surrounding area. Over the centuries, several members of the Fitzwilliam family have represented Peterborough in Parliament or influenced the choice of other candidates. The Third Earl Fitzwilliam gave the town the house in Priestgate that became Peterborough's first public infirmary. Although the title of Earl Fitzwilliam is no longer in use, Milton Hall is still the family home and the agricultural land to the west of Peterborough is mainly farmed by their tenants. When the New Town status was granted to Peterborough, about 2,000 acres of Milton land were purchased for the development of the new township of Bretton.

30 March

When Cardinal Wolsey failed to secure Henry VIII's divorce, he was forced to leave London in disgrace and retire to York, where he was still archbishop. As he travelled north, he stopped at Peterborough Abbey for two weeks. His arrival must have caused quite a stir as he brought with him twelve cartloads of belongings, including his bed. On Palm Sunday he led the procession of monks and held the Maundy Thursday service in the Lady Chapel where he washed, dried and kissed the feet of fifty-nine poor men before giving Maundy money to them. Fifty-eight received 12d, but the fifty-ninth received 2s, although there is no record of how the fortunate fifty-ninth man was chosen. In addition, each was given a pair of shoes, enough canvas to make a shirt, some bread and some herrings. One source says they had a barrel of herrings, another that they were presented with three red and three white herrings! Wolsey celebrated Easter before leaving for Milton Hall, home of the Fitzwilliams, where he had to stay in a large tent in the grounds because the king had forbidden anyone to have him under their roof!

29 January

Townspeople must have gathered at the abbey gates as Katharine of Aragon's coffin arrived from Kimbolton Castle on a wagon drawn by six horses draped in black. She had been a well-loved queen and although her divorce from Henry meant that her status reverted to princess dowager and her funeral (as well as her burial place, in the 'nearest great abbey' to Kimbolton) reflected that, it was still an impressive enough affair.

The carriage carrying Katharine's coffin was covered in black velvet with a large silver cross, and inside was a cloth of gold with a crimson cross. Sixteen priests followed the leading rider, who carried a gold cross, then came officials carrying their rods of office and heralds wearing their coats of arms. Fifty servants with burning torches came next whilst heralds and standard-bearers surrounded the wagon itself. Women mourners and members of Katharine's staff followed as the procession was met by abbots and bishops and led into the abbey where over 1,000 candles burned around the coffin as masses were said.

Henry did not allow their daughter Mary to attend the funeral and he was instead represented by his niece. Katharine's lifelong friend Maria de Salinas, now Lady Willoughby, led mourners as the former queen was buried near the steps of the altar. Katharine's life is still celebrated every year in Peterborough Cathedral.

29 November

Henry VIII's dissolution of England's monasteries took effect in Peterborough on this date when Abbot John Chambers voluntarily surrendered control of the monastery to the king, thus keeping his good favour. For the first time in nearly 900 years, the town and the lands of the Soke were not subject to the authority of St Peter's Abbey, which had even given the town its name. For a while, Chambers was known by the title of Warden of the College of Peterborough, and when Henry created a new diocese centred on Peterborough, Chambers became its first bishop.

Since the establishment of the first monastery in the seventh century, lands and privileges had been granted to the abbots of Medeshampstead (later known as Peterborough). Their power was so great that the area they controlled, the Liberty or Soke of Peterborough, was not subject to sheriff's courts, as in the counties of England. The abbot controlled justice, the gaols and all life in the town. After 1539 some powers went to the bishops and the Dean and Chapter, though the responsibility for the gaol was later given over to the new Lord Paramount of the town. Chambers' decision to give up his powers as abbot straight away probably contributed to the relatively trouble-free changes in the town.

4 September

Peterborough became a city in September 1541 by order of King Henry VIII. When Henry moved England away from the power of the Roman Catholic Church, the monasteries ceased to exist. Many were destroyed as their riches were stripped away, the buildings pulled down and the stone used elsewhere.

John Chambers, the last abbot and a Peterborough man, surrendered the abbey in 1539 and was appointed a Royal Chaplain. When Church lands were reorganised, Peterborough became the centre of a new diocese with the former abbey church becoming the cathedral and the remaining monks serving as priests here. Henry made John Chambers the first bishop and also created the City of Peterborough. This meant that, for the first time in its history, Peterborough was not subject to the abbot's rule alone and moved towards taking responsibility for its own affairs. The Dean and Chapter of the cathedral now took over some of the former abbot's administration but it would be centuries before Peterborough had an elected Corporation. Peterborough was one of only six other abbey churches, including Westminster Abbey, which survived to become cathedrals. Had it not been for Henry's decision, Peterborough might not have had the beautiful cathedral that still dominates the city today.

4 September

The King's School dates back to 1541 and was founded by Henry VIII at the same time as the old abbey church became the cathedral. There were to be eight choristers who had their own schoolmaster and twenty 'poor boys with no friends to support them but with a gift and disposition for learning' with a second schoolmaster in the new grammar school. Pupils had to be able to read and have knowledge of grammar before they were admitted. Once in attendance they would receive a Classical education and many were expected to become priests. Somewhat unfairly, the cathedral authorities could nominate boys for the available places and it seems that they often nominated their own sons.

The first schoolroom was in the Becket Chapel on the left of the cathedral gate and the seats allocated to the master and head boy can still be seen. When the premises became too small some lessons were held in the room over the cathedral gate, St Nicholas' Chapel, before King's moved, in 1885, to the buildings it now occupies in Park Road. Girls were admitted in 1976 and cathedral choristers, boys and girls, are still educated at the King's School.

26 June

It was on this date that Elizabeth I signed the first 'deed of feoffment' whereby thirteen new Feoffees, or Charitable Commissioners, were appointed. The Feoffees took charge of Peterborough's administration and, together with the Victorian Improvers, they helped run the town until the first Corporation was elected in the late nineteenth century. Previously the abbot had charge of daily life in the town and throughout the Soke. After the abbey closed, some powers passed to the Dean and Chapter of the cathedral and some to the Lord Paramount of the Soke, Lord Burghley. There was no elected Corporation, mayor, nor townspeople responsible for running public services. Three Peterborough businessmen bought back Church land that had been sold off or confiscated after the closure of the abbey. The property and income from it were handed over to trustees, or Feoffees, who had to maintain the roads, drains, bridge and organise charity for the poor. They set up a House of Correction and looked after the parish church, put up pesthouses for plague victims and ran almshouses. Food, clothing, apprenticeships and money for those left destitute are amongst the wide range of charitable donations noted in their records. Their numbers and efficiency fluctuated but generally the city functioned as far as charity and limited income allowed until 1790 when some of the Feoffees' responsibility passed to the Improvement Committee.

20 December

On this date in 1576, the title of Lord Paramount of Peterborough, then held by the Bishop of Peterborough, was passed by Queen Elizabeth I to the Marquess of Exeter, William Cecil of Burghley. Like the Fitzwilliams of Milton, the Cecils were to play an important role in the life of the city. As Lords Paramount they were involved in local government and the administration of justice, as well as being responsible for the town gaol near the cathedral gateway. The title of Lord Paramount is still held by William Cecil's descendants today.

In 1555, when William Cecil was secretary to Princess, later Queen, Elizabeth, work on his great house began. By the time his splendid home was finished in 1587, Cecil was Lord Treasurer of England and chief minister to the queen. The greatest craftsmen of the day were employed to work at Burghley and 'Capability' Brown designed the gardens in the eighteenth century.

After centuries of his family's political involvement in the city, the fourth marquess supported the Soke of Peterborough's right to be an administrative authority when changes were being made to county councils in 1888. Burghley House near Stamford is now part of Peterborough Unitary Authority and is one of the major visitor attractions in the area.

1 August

Unlike the grand public funeral procession of Katharine of Aragon fifty-one years earlier, the lead coffin containing the body of Mary, Queen of Scots arrived in darkness, having left Fotheringhay Castle at ten o'clock at night. Arriving at the town bridge at about two o'clock in the morning, the small, torch-lit procession was met by the bishop, dean and other officials who escorted it to the Bishop's Palace. The burial place was on the opposite side of the choir to the tomb of Katharine of Aragon and black cloths were hung all round the cathedral. On the night of Tuesday, 1 August, the funeral procession left the Bishop's Palace to walk to the burial site, led by 100 'poor old women' mourners who went to stand on either side of the church. The choir and singing men led the other mourners from the main door, followed by officials from the town, noble lords and ladies of Scotland and England, and officers of the dead queen, including her Roman Catholic confessor. After the sermon, Mary's former officers broke their staffs of office over their heads and threw them into the vault. Feasts were held for guests on the Monday and Tuesday nights. When Mary's son became King James VI of Scotland and James I of England, his mother's body was taken for reburial in Westminster Abbey.

2 July

Unusually for a humble citizen, Robert Scarlett was buried in the cathedral in July 1594. Scarlett claimed to have buried two generations of Peterborough families. Born in 1496, he worked as a gravedigger and was renowned for his strength, even as a boy. His main claim to fame is that he buried both Katharine of Aragon and Mary, Queen of Scots after their funerals in Peterborough Cathedral. Scarlett was employed as sexton by the parish church and he was also responsible for buying bread and wine for Communion. He had to keep the churchyard clean and ring the bells.

Records showed that Scarlett lived in the Marketstede and that he married twice; his second marriage taking place in 1585, only a year after the death of his first wife, and when Scarlett was 89 years old. He was known to enjoy telling stories of his exploits and one of those who heard him was probably the dean's son, John Fletcher, a pupil at the King's School at the cathedral gateway. Fletcher went on to write plays and worked with Shakespeare, and it is possible that Shakespeare based the character of the gravedigger in *Hamlet* upon one of Peterborough's most legendary residents and his stories.

16 April

During the English Civil War, Parliamentarian forces were sent to Crowland where a group of Royalist soldiers were holding out. They made their base in Peterborough where the commander of the first foot soldiers to arrive, Colonel Hubbard, locked the cathedral in order to protect it. Two days later a cavalry troop arrived under the command of Colonel Cromwell. They broke down the doors and rode into the cathedral, firing muskets at the ceiling and breaking windows and stone monuments. The altar was pulled over and smashed, and all the stained-glass windows were broken, including those in the cloister, which were of very high quality. Fortunately, a record of the windows and other parts of the church had been made by Simon Gunton, vicar of St John's. Documents and books were destroyed but Humphrey Austin, a minor canon at the cathedral, managed to save the valuable Chronicle of Robert of Swapham. He paid 10s to buy it from a soldier who thought it was a Latin Bible and the receipt is still in the book today. The monument over the tomb of Katharine of Aragon was broken up, as was the family memorial of the Royalist Orme family, who lived in Priestgate. The Lady Chapel was so badly damaged that it was later pulled down completely and the stone used for other building work. It was nearly 200 years before major work was carried out to restore the cathedral properly.

29 May

From prehistoric times the Peterborough area benefited from its position on the Fen Edge. In summer the land meant good pasture for animals and in winter, when the Fens flooded, animals could be moved to slightly higher land. Later, landowners wanted to take advantage of the rich agricultural land by draining the Fens to reduce flooding and extend their lands.

The Car Dyke seems to have been a Roman project to take water off the fields. Morton's Leam was built in the fifteenth century with the aim of changing the course of the River Nene by diverting water to a parallel channel. An Act of Parliament on the above date cleared the way. Dutch engineers such as Cornelius Vermuyden were brought to England to undertake large-scale works in the Fens and were promised a share in the land that they drained. People who had previously enjoyed common use of pastures and resources opposed the enclosure of the new farmland, which robbed them of their livelihoods. In fact, the embankment of rivers and use of wind pumps were not efficient enough to dry out the land, creating new problems as the peat shrank. Once more efficient pumps were developed the Fens became productive agricultural land and the risk of flooding was reduced. Peterborough's Embankment is now an attractive leisure area and the site of the Key Theatre.

30 August

Oliver Cromwell's Lord Chief Justice, Oliver St John, bought the lease of Longthorpe Manor in Peterborough when Church lands were sold off during the Civil War. He built Thorpe Hall on his land, using stone from the damaged cathedral, supposedly given in gratitude by the people of Peterborough for saving the cathedral from complete destruction. The stone certainly came from the ruins of the Lady Chapel, which was demolished at the time, having been damaged beyond repair by Cromwell's troops. Some of the stone was used to restore other parts of the building and the rest used in the construction of St John's new house. Actual evidence of stone from the cathedral was only found during later building work as carvings had been turned inwards to hide their origins.

Thorpe Hall was built between 1653 and 1658 and is one of only a handful of great houses built during the Commonwealth before the monarchy returned to England in the person of Charles II. St John refused to take part in the trial of Charles I, though he was a leading Parliamentarian. His son Francis later became one of Peterborough's Members of Parliament.

John Evelyn described Thorpe Hall as a 'stately place, built out of the ruins of the Bishop's Palace and Cloister' when he visited at the end of August 1654. Thorpe Hall is now a Sue Ryder Hospice.

16 September

Outbreaks of plague occurred many times but the most severe began when a visitor from London brought the infection into the town on this date. The events of those years were recorded by the priest of St John's parish church, Simon Gunton, who was the only priest not to leave Peterborough in order to escape infection. Attempts to stop the spread of the disease by shutting up the houses where someone was ill were unsuccessful and few families escaped sickness or death. At the height of the plague, 160 people died during the month of July alone and burial grounds could not keep up with the number of deaths. Some were buried on their own property or near the 'Pest House' for plague victims, which was in the Westgate area of the town, as well as in the town's churchyard. The pest houses were wooden buildings erected as needed by the Feoffees. When not in use, the wood was stored in St John's church. Simon Gunton recorded the burials in his parish register and added comments at the bottom of the pages, such as 'Simon Gunton, saved by the grace of God'. By the time of the last death in May 1667, a third of the population had died, but this seems to have been the last occasion the pest houses were needed in Peterborough.

19 June

Following eleven years of Republican rule, a public subscription was set up in Peterborough to celebrate the coronation of Charles II in 1660. The money was used for one of Peterborough's most notable buildings, the Guildhall, which was completed in 1671. Minutes of a meeting held there on 19 June show the amount still owed to the architect, John Lovin. Also known as the Butter Cross or Market Cross, the various names recall some of its uses through the years. A market cross would have stood in the centre of the market place – now Cathedral Square – from the Middle Ages. Butter, eggs and poultry were sold under the arches until 1926 when the market moved to its present location. The chamber above the arches has been used for several purposes but mainly as Peterborough's Town Hall and Council Chamber until 1933. To accommodate the council offices, there was a house attached to the west side of the Guildhall, which was demolished in 1964. Earl Fitzwilliam paid £20 towards the £300 needed to complete the new building and insisted that the royal coat of arms should be displayed in a prominent position. The coats of arms of the bishop, dean and two influential local families, the Ormes and Montagus, were added.

19 August

Thomas Deacon was a wealthy local wool merchant known for his generosity to the poor of Peterborough. On his death on 19 August 1721, he left most of his property to be used for charitable works, including the setting up of a school. Twenty poor boys were to be clothed and taught to read, write and 'cast accounts' before becoming apprenticed to a trade. Upon leaving they were to be given a suit of clothes and a Bible.

Whereas the King's School taught Latin and Greek, the opening of Deacon's establishment gave poorer boys an education that would prepare them for more practical work on leaving school. The majority of charity or 'Dame' schools in the early eighteenth century taught very basic skills in writing, reading and arithmetic, and attendance was not compulsory. Although a Mrs Ireland had given £100 for a free school for ten boys and ten girls, Thomas Deacon had seen the need for apprentices and his school was to provide them. Mrs Ireland's School closed in 1839 and the boys went to Deacon's while the girls joined St John's Middle Class School. The Thomas Deacon Trust still partially funds the new academy for about 2,000 students in Queen's Road.

27 June

Edward Wortley Montagu served twice as Member of Parliament for Peterborough, from 1734 to 1747 and from 1754 to 1761. During his first term of office, on 27 June 1744, he gave a newly built house and land in Westgate and Cowgate to the city, to be used as an almshouse. Although he had a reputation for not liking to spend his money, his generous gift meant that more of the city's poor could be housed and he stated that the property was 'for the better accommodation of the poor of St John's parish'. The Feoffees ran the establishment in addition to the almshouses in Cumbergate.

The new Poor Law of 1834 introduced more rules for the management of workhouses and set up Boards of Guardians to run them. The Board of Guardians originally intended to take over the Westgate workhouse from the Feoffees but met great opposition. In fact, the new rules meant that there would have to be major changes in the building itself to provide the required separate accommodation for men, women and children. By 1837 the old workhouse had been converted into a row of almshouses. Charles Dickens visited the Westgate workhouse before writing *Oliver Twist*.

15 March

Matthew Wyldebore, a former Member of Parliament for the town, left money for the bell-ringers of St John's church provided that they rang a peal in his memory every year on the anniversary of his death. The fifteenth day of March therefore became known as Wyldebore Day and the tradition has continued since 1781. His will stated that the minister should decide whether the bell-ringers would receive the bequest partly in money and partly in 'entertainment'. Although he also asked that a sermon be preached that day, the tradition has lapsed.

Wyldebore was grateful to the bell-ringers of St John's for guiding him home when he was lost in a thick fog on the edge of the Fens. Peterborough was such a small town, surrounded by marshy land and open common land; it would be easy to lose one's path if a Fenland mist came down suddenly. Wyldebore knew that he could easily have drowned if the sound of the bells had not guided him safely back to town.

Although Wyldebore represented Peterborough in Parliament his reputation was not good. In the 1774 elections his rival James Phipps accused him of bribery and corruption, claiming that some of the votes had been cast by people who were not entitled to take part in the election, whilst other eligible ratepayers had been prevented from voting. Some people were prepared to believe the accusations and political cartoons of the time implied that in 1768 Wyldebore had paid another candidate to withdraw. However, when the case came to be heard, Phipps withdrew his charge of bribery and Wyldebore was able to take up office.

4 May

The birthday of Lord Milton, son of Lord and Lady Fitzwilliam, was celebrated in style at the Angel Inn on Narrow Bridge Street. The event was, in some ways, a public occasion, even if the closest most townspeople got to the happy event was the street outside the inn. The day's festivities got underway at eleven in the morning with a public breakfast and the arrival of the guests, who no doubt gave the onlookers plenty of opportunity to gossip about their fancy clothes and appearance. The newspaper reports that the ladies were wearing white and straw-coloured ribbons that gave the effect of 'the most elegant neatness'. After breakfast, there was dancing until three o'clock when the ladies left, apparently through a crowd of admiring spectators. Presumably the ladies returned after dressing for the remainder of the evening. Dinner was served at four and toasts were drunk to the health of the king, Lord Milton and his family amongst others. By eight o'clock in the evening, the ballroom was full again and dancing carried on till one in the morning. The report concludes with the fervent hope that there would always be a Lord Milton in the Fitzwilliam family.

21 January

By the end of the eighteenth century, it was becoming more difficult for the Feoffees and city governors to finance and meet all the civic needs of a growing population. Owing to the lack of a town Corporation, the work of maintaining the city's streets and drains and administering parish charities was still the responsibility of the Feoffees, as it had been since the mid-sixteenth century, and local people were demanding that action be taken to improve the running of the town.

An Act of Parliament on this date established the Peterborough Pavement and Improvement Commissioners to take over some of the responsibilities of the Feoffees. The Commissioners therefore effectively ran local government until the end of the nineteenth century. The Act had noted that public streets were 'not properly paved, repaired, cleaned, lighted and watched' and the first thirty-three Commissioners began work to rectify this immediately. The initial reaction to the new Commissioners was not completely favourable, however. Local press reports pointed out that paving stones were laid outside properties belonging to the Commissioners and their associates, improving their businesses first. Rates were levied on some properties and toll bars were set up to raise money. The Boongate area of the city, too poor to raise rates, was not improved. The Minster Precincts, outside the parish of St John's, claimed they did not need improving.

10 January

At a meeting in the Angel Inn on the above date, the Agricultural Association was founded to share knowledge and improve methods of farming and breeding livestock at a time of great change in English life. As the Industrial Revolution drew workers from the countryside into the towns, the increasing population meant that farmers needed to generate more food, more economically, for those who did not grow produce of their own. Enclosure Acts allowed landowners to fence off large areas of open fields and common land on which villagers used to graze animals, grow small amounts of crops or harvest naturally growing plants to supplement their diet. Land could now be used more efficiently, particularly with the developments in agricultural machinery.

From 1836 the Peterborough Agricultural Association began to widen its membership. Their shows began to attract non-farming members of the public and, besides the competitions involving best livestock and new machinery, other entertainment was provided. Emphasising Peterborough's mix of agriculture and industry, the Agricultural Show was first held in the centre of town in the yard behind the Wagon and Horses pub, where Bridge Street crosses Bourges Boulevard today. As the town and show expanded it moved to Boroughbury then Millfield and eventually out to the site at Alwalton where the last East of England Show took place in 2013.

7 April

The world's first purpose-built prisoner-of-war camp began to receive inmates in April 1797. Norman Cross, situated outside Peterborough near the Great North Road, was built to house French soldiers and sailors who had been captured at sea during the war against Napoleon. Far enough away from access to ports but with local resources able to supply the new camp, Norman Cross housed more than 5,000 inmates at any one time. The prisoners were usually brought by boat along the River Nene and disembarked in town, before marching out to Norman Cross. The huge demand for food and supplies was a big boost to Peterborough's economy. The local basket and hat making industry was at first threatened by prisoners being allowed to sell such goods at markets held outside the camp. When this trade was officially stopped, prisoners began to make models from straw or animal bone. Examples of their skill can be seen in Peterborough Museum. Although their diet included fresh meat and vegetables, crowded conditions, together with prisoners' obsession with gambling away the smallest luxury, even food, meant that disease spread quickly. During a cholera epidemic, 1,000 men died. The camp closed in 1814 after Napoleon's defeat.

1 January

In 1798, Henry Walker of Westgate was chosen by the Committee for the Management of Sedan Chairs to control the operation of sedan chairs in the city. In most other areas of Britain the use of sedan chairs died out during the early part of the nineteenth century, but in Peterborough they continued to be popular until the 1860s. Some of the chairs were in very poor repair and the chairmen were not always reliable. Many did not keep good time and some were accused of being scruffy, rude, or even drunk when they were working. Henry Walker's job was to organise all the sedan chair operators and to improve and maintain standards of service. There were to be set charges, starting from 1s for a dinner or tea visit to 1s 6d to be taken to an assembly or ball. Further charges were incurred if the chairmen were kept waiting. Liveried porters made the service more popular as ladies wanted to arrive in style at social functions. Peterborough's roads were in a bad state, muddy, dirty and narrow, which is why sedans were popular long after they had disappeared from other towns. Improvements made to the sedan chairs at the end of the eighteenth century ensured they were a necessary addition to Peterborough life for another seventy years.

1 August

Peterborough's agricultural workers were all affected by enclosure, particularly after a parliamentary Act of August 1809. Enclosure was the fencing off or taking over by landowners of land that had previously been 'common' land. Rights of access to common land gave those living in the parish a way of supplementing their income. Animals could be put to pasture, food such as berries and nuts could be picked and firewood gathered. Although at least half of England's countryside had been 'enclosed' by the nineteenth century, the 1809 Act of Parliament made it easier for landowners to fence off or sell land for private use. As agriculture developed and more food needed to be produced, it made economic sense to farm the land in a new way. Drainage and better crop management improved the land and animals could be kept and bred to improve the stock. It was not until about 1820 that some villages round Peterborough felt the full effect of the 1809 law. John Clare, 'the peasant poet' from Helpston, witnessed the changes to traditional rural life. Many of those who were driven off the land ended up in Peterborough workhouses.

18 May

The last public hanging in Peterborough was witnessed by a crowd of about 6,000 people in May 1812. David Myers, a draper from Stamford, was convicted of committing a homosexual act in Burghley Park. The jury returned a guilty verdict within five minutes of retiring. Despite an appeal to the Prince Regent to withdraw the death penalty, local papers reported that the verdict gave 'universal satisfaction'. Myers accepted his fate and spent his last hours in prayer after a tearful farewell to his wife, by whom he had six children. He requested that his coffin be left in his cell on the eve of the execution and that his last letter from his wife be placed in the coffin after his death. A clergyman travelled in the carriage with him as he was driven to the gallows and throughout the journey he appeared calm, even 'happy'. Despite travelling to witness the execution, most of the spectators were said to be moved to tears by his final prayers on the scaffold. After telling them to 'take warning by his example', David Myers became the last person whose execution in Peterborough provided a morbid form of 'entertainment' for his fellow citizens.

23 April

The last recorded public flogging in Peterborough took place in the market place as late as 1819. The *Stamford Mercury* of 23 April reported that Benjamin Ayres and John Wyles were found guilty of stealing malt from Mr Edward Hall of Wansford at Peterborough Sessions on Wednesday, 20 April. Both were sentenced to be publicly whipped – a form of punishment that dated back to the Middle Ages and was administered by the town's constable. 'Whipping at the cart's tail' meant that the prisoner was stripped to the waist and made to kneel at the back of an open cart. He would be dragged around the market place and whipped whilst crowds looked on. More than one circuit of the market place could be made depending on the seriousness of the crime. Physical pain and humiliation were hallmarks of many of the sentences handed out until more humane forms of punishment were gradually preferred in a more enlightened age. Ward constables had been appointed for each area of Peterborough for centuries but the Improvement Commissioners set up a new group for policing the city in 1836. It was not until 1874, however, that the town gained a modern police force.

7 November

Edmund Artis, agent to the Fitzwilliam family of Milton, excavated sites around Castor church over several years. In the book recording his finds, he notes that a mosaic floor was discovered on the above date.

Finds of mosaics, wall paintings and bathhouses show that the area prospered in Roman times. The grandest building dates from the mid-third century and dwarfs all other villas in the area. Its position, overlooking the site of the Roman town of Durobrivae, the River Nene and the surrounding country-side, together with the extent of the construction, indicate that it must have been an important residence. The palatial size of the building (nearly 275m long and 122m wide) has led archaeologists to suggest that it was the base, or praetorium, of a high-ranking Roman official.

The strategic importance of the area on the edge of the Fens to the east, together with lines of communication that passed through and close by present-day Castor, would have provided an excellent base for a powerful military commander. Whoever lived there may have been responsible for controlling a vast imperial estate which extended across the Fens. The ruins lie buried under the area surrounding the church of St Kyneburgha, though traces of Roman walls can be seen in the village.

12 June

One of the most popular events in the nineteenth century was watching hot-air balloons soar into the air. In June, Peterborough enjoyed 'one of the greatest treats witnessed here' when a Mr Green set off on a flight in his hot-air balloon. Some 800 people gathered to watch the balloon soar up 'to a great height'. It drifted off towards Eye before landing near Spalding and Mr Green was given a large breakfast before returning to Peterborough in a chaise. In total, the paper reported that upwards of 15,000 people saw the balloon in flight. In the previous month, carriages had brought many spectators to Peterborough to witness an earlier ascent by Mr Green. Large crowds gathered next to the gas works to watch him make his 149th flight. The wind was so strong that it was not until seven o'clock in the evening that he climbed into his balloon. A gentleman who was meant to go with him had to stay behind as the balloon was only about two-thirds inflated. As the balloon rose, a band struck up 'God Save the King' and everyone cheered. Around 200 people were watching from a tent and about 1,000 more watched from the surrounding roads. After being blown off course a few times, the balloon eventually landed near March. (Image source: LC-USZ62-131843)

2 September

The great Edmund Kean was due to perform at Peterborough's theatre on 2 September 1830 in the role of Richard III. The theatre, which was next to St John's church on the site later occupied by the Corn Exchange, was packed with people eager to see England's most famous Shakespearean actor. Unfortunately, the audience were disappointed to find that the role was to be played by an understudy as Edmund Kean was ill. On the following Saturday huge numbers of people filled the theatre again, this time looking forward to seeing Kean's performance as Shylock in the *Merchant of Venice*. Sixteen years earlier he had made his debut at Drury Lane in London in a performance that was hailed as one of the greatest ever seen. Although he did appear on this occasion it was reported that everyone was disappointed as Keane was obviously still not well and performed badly. This was possibly the same play attended by the poet John Clare, who went there as the guest of Bishop Marsh and his wife. His mental health had deteriorated and, not being able to distinguish between reality and acting, he attempted to attack 'Shylock' believing that he was a genuine villain. If this were the case, perhaps it was not surprising that Edmund Kean did not display his great acting abilities to the full!

28 January

This day's issue of the *Huntingdon, Bedford and Peterborough Gazette* included a report about a charity in Peterborough known as the Mendicity Society. 'Mendicants' or beggars who may just be passing through the town, were not catered for by the existing charities and, as such, the society sought to move beggars off the streets and provide them with food and a bed for the night. This not only provided help for those with no source of income but also pleased townspeople by clearing the streets at night.

Assuming it would be easier to raise money by many small donations instead of a few large ones, 250 subscribers made one-off donations of £35 and other subscribers gave up to £80 a month, including £30 from the parish. Thanks to the generosity of Lord Fitzwilliam, a lodging house provided cleaner and airier accommodation than had been available before. On the first six nights, seventy-two people were provided with food and lodging and others were given bread and potatoes. During the month preceding the newspaper report, over 200 people received help. At a time when the parish also ran workhouses, the numbers of those needing help reflects society at the time.

23 February

A large part of the centre of town was destroyed in a huge blaze that swept through the Westgate area, fanned by strong winds. Rumours suggested that it had started in a Mr Spriggs' house, where his lodger, 'Nottingham Frank', had been trying to tar rope by melting tar over a fire in an outbuilding. Sparks blew through chinks in the chimney and set the thatched roof alight, but the blaze immediately spread to nearby properties. Many buildings in the upper part of Westgate had been completely destroyed before the fire service arrived. Squire's Brewery came under threat but was saved – though the ale had already been moved out of harm's way by willing volunteers! Most people worked hard to save the rest of the town, but newspaper reports mention that some took the chance to get very drunk. One old lady died and others were badly burned, a remarkably small number considering the extent of the fire. Sixty houses, mainly thatched, were completely destroyed and others badly damaged. Eighty families, about 200 people, were made homeless. Temporary accommodation was found for them and the townspeople rallied round with soup, bread and potatoes and a fund was set up to help the victims.

3 December

The Peterborough Poor Law Union was formed in 1835 to oversee the changes in the administration of workhouses brought about by the new Poor Laws. Workhouses were now required to separate men, women and children so the town's existing workhouses and almshouses were inadequate. The new Union Workhouse was built in 1836 on Thorpe Road for 200 inmates, but by 1874 there were over 370 residents. People were admitted at their own request and were subject to a humiliating process before they entered. Their own clothes were taken and then they were washed and given workhouse clothing. A diet was assigned to each person, depending on their age and sex, and the number of the diet they were given was pinned to their clothes. The regime was designed to discourage residents from remaining in the workhouse but many had little option. As time went on, the majority of residents were either elderly or infirm, or children who were orphaned or abandoned. An infirmary was added along with schoolrooms so that children could be given a basic education; boys were apprenticed to local tradesmen and girls were sent into service. A new infirmary section, added in 1920, became St John's building on the Memorial Hospital site. The workhouse closed in 1930.

23 April

The foundation stone for the new gaol on Thorpe Road was laid by Earl Fitzwilliam and remained the town's gaol until 1878. The former entrance and courtroom of the gaol is now the Sessions House restaurant. Justices of the Peace heard cases at the quarter sessions held in the front part of the prison, which was known as the Liberty Gaol because it was under the jurisdiction of the Liberty of Peterborough. Prior to the Thorpe Road building there had been two small prisons in Peterborough. The Bridewell, which stood next to Cumbergate, was run by the Feoffees and housed those who had committed minor crimes. The other gaol was next to the cathedral gate, where it had been the responsibility of the abbot in the days of the monastery before passing to the control of Lord Exeter of Burghley. Both prisons were in a very poor condition and prisoners had escaped as the one in the Precincts in particular was not secure. After 1878, prisoners were sent to Northampton or to Cambridge. The gaol itself was demolished in 1961 and the magistrates' court is now in Bridge Street. The current Peterborough Prison opened in 2005 on the site of the old Baker Perkins works.

2 June

The first train into Peterborough, along the new line from Northampton, steamed into East Station near Fair Meadows on a sunny day in June 1845. Coaches had brought spectators into town to witness the arrival of the first passenger service. Fearing for their livelihoods, local coach drivers had been doing their best to put people off railways by warning of the high-speed accidents that were bound to occur. They did not deter the thousands who turned out to see the train or those who crowded into the carriages at every stop on the way. By the time the train left Wansford, passengers were riding on top of the coaches. Staff had difficulty persuading them to stoop as the train passed under the bridges, so that they were not knocked off! At the end of the journey, a brass band played and the bells of the town's churches rang out. About 8,000 people were waiting to see the train, more than the city's whole population. Although huge crowds were celebrating the future of transport in this area, not everyone was happy. Some thought that cathedral services would be interrupted by the noise of the engines letting off steam. East Station finally closed to passenger trains in 1966.

23 September

Surrounded by some of the best agricultural land in the country, Peterborough was at the centre of trade in cereal crops in the nineteenth century. Local dealers bought the old theatre on Church Street in 1846 and built the Corn Exchange at a cost of £5,500, to capitalise on the increasing wealth coming into the city from local farmland. The architect designed the building 'in an Italian style', big enough to hold 1,000 people, which made it suitable not only for sales, but also for all sorts of public gatherings. The opening dinner was held on 24 September 1848 and tickets, costing 12s 6d, included a bottle of wine and dessert! The Exchange was one of the busiest in the country and hosted many events over the years, including tea parties at times of public celebrations, such as the 1863 wedding of the Prince of Wales to Princess Alexandra. Charles Dickens gave several readings here and in 1861 it was the headquarters for a week-long meeting of the Archaeological Society of England. In 1942 the building was badly damaged by firebombs. Dances were held there until it was demolished at the beginning of the 1960s.

25 October

A local newspaper reported that Whittlesey Mere, once the largest expanse of fresh water in southern England, had disappeared. Although the mere had become quite shallow and was completely surrounded by reed beds, it was a still a favourite area for boating, fishing, wildfowling and skating in winter. After many years of failed attempts to drain the land, local landowners who were determined to exploit the agricultural potential of this vast area made plans to use a new type of pump. The newly invented steam pump had been on show that year at the Great Exhibition in London and could drain 1,600 gallons of water (70 tons) per minute. Local people went to watch as the mere was gradually drained and they collected the fish that had been left stranded as the water disappeared. Other objects that had sunk centuries before were revealed as time went on, including a silver censer or incense burner, possibly from Ramsey Abbey and dating from the fourteenth century. Rich agricultural land replaced the mere but took away some local livelihoods and leisure activities enjoyed for hundreds of years.

2 June

The infirmary in Priestgate opened its doors in 1857 and was the city's hospital until 1928. On the above date Earl Fitzwilliam gave the building, now the museum, to replace the small public dispensary and lodging house in Milton Street. Although the lodging house became known as the infirmary, it simply provided short-term accommodation for people who had come for medicine and provided no other services at first. The original funding for the first public dispensary had come from money saved when the Peterborough Defence Corps was disbanded after the Napoleonic Wars. Until 1816 only the rich could afford the services of a doctor so even limited healthcare was an improvement. The Priestgate premises had outpatient facilities and kitchens on the ground floor and wards upstairs. Operations were carried out in the ward until 1894 when an operating theatre was built. Dr Thomas Walker was surgeon from 1862 until 1906 and was made an honorary freeman of the city in recognition of his work. Alfred Taylor was hospital secretary and his work led to Peterborough having one of the first X-ray machines in the country. Later extensions to the building improved conditions and increased the number of patients able to be treated.

21 December

When the Great Northern Railway Company applied to build twenty cottages in December 1856, few could have realised how dramatically the town would start to change. The small market town of 3,000 residents in the early nineteenth century was transformed by the arrival of the railway and the industrial development associated with it. Within a few years, four major railway companies had arrived in Peterborough, bringing not only jobs for locals but also skilled workers from other parts of the country to operate and build the railways. Peterborough's existing housing could not cope with the sudden growth in population so railway companies began to build accommodation for their employees and the town expanded along the line of the railway. The Great Northern Railway Company built in the area now known as New England and provided not just housing, but a 'new town'. The terraced houses enjoyed better conditions than many existing properties, with gas and piped water supplied by the railway company. Schools, shops, churches, pubs and a school for apprentices made New England a small town within a town. Houses at the end of the terrace were sometimes larger and accommodated more senior workers such as guards or engine drivers. The rows of railway houses, known locally as 'The Barracks', were mostly demolished when Bourges Boulevard was built, though some still remain on Lincoln Road.

18 October

An evening spent listening to the great Charles Dickens was obviously a highlight of social life in the city in the mid-nineteenth century. He described the Corn Exchange, where the performance took place, as very pretty, 'large, bright and cheerful and wonderfully well lighted'. Dickens made several visits to Peterborough as he toured the country giving readings of his work.

The night of 18 October 1859 was particularly special as he described the audience as 'the finest I have ever read to'. The compliments were welcome because on another occasion he claimed not to like the town itself, describing it very unkindly as 'like the back door to some other place. It is, I should hope, the deadest and most utterly inert little town in the British dominions.' Despite those comments, he visited on several other occasions. In Peterborough's favour, he thought the front of the cathedral 'the loveliest I ever saw'. Though he gave more than one reading during his visit in 1859, he noted that twice as many people were turned away as could get tickets. The audience was treated to the sight of Dickens in full evening dress, with buttonhole and purple waistcoat, no doubt an occasion they talked about for years.

24 June

Peterscourt was originally a teacher-training college for men, run by the Diocese of Peterborough. It is the best example of Victorian architecture in the city centre and was designed by Sir George Gilbert Scott who also built the Albert Memorial and the hotel at St Pancras Station in London. The red-brick building has tall Tudor-style chimneys and originally had a small schoolroom built at the side so that the students could practice their classroom skills. A house for the principal was at one end of the building. The training college closed in 1914 but was reopened in 1921 to train women teachers. Photographs show landscaped gardens backing on to the cathedral grounds – these have unfortunately disappeared under a car park. Peterscourt ceased to be a teacher training college in 1936. It had a new lease of life as the American Servicemen's Club in the Second World War, attracting airmen from bases around Peterborough, including Clark Gable. Perkins Engines used the building as offices and Frank Perkins brought the seventeenth-century carved doorway from the bomb-damaged London Guildhall. Peterscourt was not the only example of George Gilbert's Scott's work in Peterborough. He also carried out restoration work in the cathedral.

7 December

In 1872 the town celebrated the opening of the first iron bridge to replace the wooden one first built in 1308 by Abbot Godfrey. For over 500 years the wooden bridge built on stone piers had been the means of crossing the River Nene into Peterborough. Constant repairs had not much improved the original narrow structure, despite the increase and weight of traffic using it. Upkeep of the bridge had always depended on charity, donations or collections, usually administered by the Feoffees, who had had the responsibility since the Middle Ages. Even the Victorian Improvement Commissioners did not take on the full repair of the bridge. Finally money was raised by public subscription to build an iron bridge, though it was still not very wide. The chaotic opening ceremony did not bode well for the bridge's future and it had to be rebuilt in the 1930s. The great civic procession that set off along Bridge Street to the opening ceremony found its way blocked by a huge crowd. Much pushing and jostling followed before Mr Ward Hunt declared the bridge open; the grand occasion fell even flatter when the first vehicle to cross over it was a rag-and-bone man's cart!

17 March

Peterborough's Charter of Incorporation, which came into effect on this date, heralded a period of rapid development in civic works. A major cause of concern was the town's water supply.

Until 1879, Peterborough's water supply came from wells located around the centre of the town. In the seventeenth century the wells became the responsibility of the Feoffees, the men chosen to oversee the distribution of charitable donations that paid for civic works. Their records show the filthy state of the wells, which provided drinking water on one side of the street, whilst open drains ran through culverts on the other side. People were paid to clear out the rubbish that accumulated in the water, including dead animals, but poor drainage meant that sewage often contaminated the drinking water, especially during periods of heavy rain and floods. This insanitary situation spread diseases such as cholera, typhus and also malaria, which was common until the Fens were drained and fewer mosquitoes were breeding close to town on Whittlesey Mere. Ignorance and lack of funds meant that nothing changed even when the population increased. In 1790 there were about 3,000 inhabitants but by 1850, over 8,500. The town's first Corporation made it a priority to find fresh sources of water that could supply Peterborough's needs. In 1879 water from Braceborough was piped into the city and from 1880 better waste disposal dramatically improved health in Peterborough.

20 May

After the Dissolution of the Monasteries, the Dean and Chapter of the new cathedral took over as Lords of the Manor of Peterborough. They owned the rights to hold markets and fairs, and they and the Feoffees carried out other duties that would have fallen to a local council, had there been one. The Feoffees had been responsible for such things as charitable works, poor houses and roads since the Middle Ages, with Improvement Commissioners taking on other responsibilities in the late eighteenth century. No opportunity really existed for residents in general to influence public works, as there was no common system of local government. Townspeople had campaigned for a mayor and Corporation who would take responsibility for the better running of the town, for improvements to roads, drainage system and water supplies, and also the upkeep of the river, gas supply and railways. The election of Peterborough's first council was held on 20 May 1874 and the first mayor was Henry Pearson Gates. On his death, a memorial was erected in Market Square, though this was moved to its present site in Bishop's Gardens in 1963.

1 April

Central Park opened at Easter 1877, although it was not completely finished at the time. The creation of walks, gardens and public sports facilities was an important addition to the town at a time when most people spent their working life in the new industries that had sprung up with the arrival of railways in Peterborough. The park was built away from the town centre and planned as part of a larger development of houses, like similar projects such as Regent's Park in London. The original design was dropped as being too expensive but the park became, as intended, an important leisure facility, especially at weekends. There were shrubberies to stroll through, trees providing shade in summer and plenty of seats where people could sit and enjoy the flowerbeds. There were spaces to play tennis, cricket and croquet, and the bandstand at the meeting point of the four main paths was a popular choice when concerts were given. There was a small pond, a rockery and a sunken garden, all features of Victorian gardens. Over the years there have been a few changes to the layout of Central Park, incorporating children's play areas, for example, but its popularity as a leisure facility remains.

23 June

Before the late nineteenth century, brick making was a seasonal industry based on small local clay pits. For the most part, the brick pits would be used as the need arose for local building work. Clay would be dug during the winter months, left to weather and then moulded in the summer. The time and labour involved meant that bricks were generally not produced in great numbers, nor were they usually transported very far from where they were dug. On this date in 1877, land at Fletton was sold and brick making developed, revolutionised by the use of clay from lower levels and the use of a new type of kiln that meant bricks could be made more quickly and cheaply all year round. The railways were soon moving millions of bricks around the country, especially to London. In 1900 the London Brick Company was formed and mergers saw the industry grow until they became one of Peterborough's major employers. In the 1950s the company advertised for workers in Italy and many families moved into the local area, forming an Italian community that still exists to this day. Excavations of the lower clay also revealed many fossil remains, particularly of marine creatures.

18 August

Peterborough's Gala and Sports Day in 1877 drew huge crowds of locals and visitors alike, all determined to make the most of a day off work. The town witnessed its busiest day for years as people came on special trains to the fête organised by Stoodley and Harmston, circus owners. Even the workhouse residents were given tickets to see the show in the big top. In addition to the circus, there were races starting with a balloon race at two o'clock and continuing with running and horse or pony races. Horse and pony racing had always been popular in the area and in the past race days had attracted rich and poor alike. The Peterborough Amateur Bicycling Club had been formed three years earlier and cycle racing was another favourite spectator sport, especially with prizes on offer. The Band of the Royal Irish Lancers had also come to entertain the crowds. The new bathing area on the Nene charged 3*d* for a day, with 1*d* extra for a towel, and the river would be busy with boats. Central Park had been open for a few months and people would stroll out to enjoy the gardens and a concert at the bandstand. For those who wanted to go further afield, there was a special train excursion to Skegness.

5 April

Work began on taking down and completely rebuilding the pillars supporting the central tower of the cathedral. Years before, a wooden platform had been erected to stop falling masonry crashing down from above and the stone pillars were cracked open in places. Wooden supports, held by metal bands around the pillars, were all that prevented the collapse of the tower and could not do the job much longer. Architect J.L. Pearson realised that rebuilding should begin from the foundations and workmen began removing the damaged columns stone by stone, numbering them as they went so that they could be put back in place more easily. New foundations were dug to give a solid base that would support the central tower. The transept ceilings were repaired and other work was undertaken which resulted in the changes that are seen today. New choir stalls, the bishop's throne and pulpit were installed and the marble canopy over the high altar (the baldacchino) was built. The organ was moved and the marble mosaic pavement was laid down by Italian workmen employed by Pearson. There was some discussion as to whether the tower should be rebuilt in a different style but the decision of the Archbishop of Canterbury was that it should be the same.

5 December

Peterborough Volunteer Fire Brigade is unique in having been manned solely by unpaid volunteers since it was founded. In May 1884 there was a serious fire at the infirmary in Priestgate and, although fortunately no one lost their life that day, the poor response of the city's fire brigade caused great concern about its ability to deal with an emergency. Local businessmen, no doubt worried about their property should there be another fire, held a meeting on 4 December in the Angel Inn on Narrow Bridge Street to set up a Volunteer Fire Brigade that would back up the regular firefighters. The use of volunteers was nothing new and in the past they had manned the pumps in return for beer – one volunteer actually starting fires to claim his drink! The new volunteer service would be more organised, however, with twelve firemen serving under a captain, along with two lieutenants. Regular occupations of the volunteers included brewers, a dentist and two vets. 'Ready and Willing' became their motto and they were soon called into action at a brewery fire in Priestgate and, as time went on, they became known for arriving quickly when needed. Funds were raised locally to provide better equipment and today volunteers continue to work alongside the regular fire service. In 1984 the Volunteer Fire Brigade received the Freedom of the City in recognition of its work.

25 June

One of the biggest celebrations ever held in Peterborough was for the Golden Jubilee of Queen Victoria. A public holiday was declared and glorious weather greeted the huge crowds gathering for the start of the day's festivities at nine in the morning. Bells rang out from the city churches before a thanksgiving service was held in St John's in the market place. There was a regatta on the Nene and five bands provided the entertainment for the crowds around the town centre and surrounding streets, which were decorated with red, white and blue flags, and bunting and lights for the evening. A meal for 1,200 'aged poor' was held in one of the only buildings big enough to accommodate them – the Midland Railway Company sheds on Thorpe Road. Even the workhouse inmates enjoyed a roast dinner, followed by plum pudding and ale. Some 5,000 school-children sang a Jubilee hymn before joining a procession led by 100 cyclists and civic dignitaries. Bands played and morris dancers were pulled along on an open wagon as the parade made its way through town to the Millfield showground where sports and tea awaited the children, each of whom was given a Jubilee mug as a memento.

7 January

On the freezing cold night of 7 January, the Congregational Chapel on Westgate, originally built in 1859, was destroyed in a huge fire.

At eleven o'clock on this Saturday night the furnaces had been stoked up to warm the church for the Sunday service. Although a policeman had passed by on his beat, he had not associated the light in the church with a fire. It appears that the underground furnace overheated and fire spread rapidly up through the floor. The alarm was raised at about three in the morning and firemen from the nearby station had arrived within seven minutes. Unfortunately, by half-past three the wooden fittings were ablaze and the roof collapsed. Both the regular fire brigade and the Volunteer Brigade worked hard to prevent the fire spreading to surrounding buildings. It was so cold that fires had to be lit round the water hydrants and the soaked clothes of the firemen began to freeze, despite the flames. Nothing could be saved from the inferno and the damage was estimated at about £4,000. The chapel had been big enough to hold 700 people and the congregation were able to move back into their church in July 1892, after rebuilding works were completed.

29 March

The storm on 29 March 1895 came after what was known in East Anglia as the 'Twelve Weeks Frost', when frozen rivers and marshes provided a perfect environment for ice skating but caused great problems for farmers. Every area of the city was affected by the 'cyclone' and few buildings escaped without any damage, particularly churches. Three turrets on the pinnacles of the west front of the cathedral toppled down, leaving one of them leaning against the west tower. Lead was also dislodged from the cathedral roof. A pinnacle was blown off St John's church in Market Square and the gable ends of houses were badly damaged. People were blown off their feet and several were seriously injured by falling masonry while a number of factory chimneys were blown over causing problems for industry. Around 200 trees were blown down at Milton and the famous 'family' of silver birches, 'the finest in England', was completely destroyed at the estate of the Marquis of Huntly at Orton Longueville. The top of Stanground church steeple broke off and repairs left the distinctive black tip that can be seen today. Waves washed over the top of Town Bridge and the meadows were flooded. However, local builders, glaziers and tilers were happy!

7 August

There was a long-standing tradition in Peterborough that when elections were over, the 'hustings' (wooden structures used for candidates' speeches) were taken away from Market Square by the crowds. The enthusiasm of the spectators, fuelled by alcohol in many cases, led to fighting as people rushed to dismantle the speakers' platform. The police tried unsuccessfully to hold back the mob and the resulting battles provided entertainment for those who had gathered at windows overlooking the town centre.

By 1895 the new sport was to kick lighted tar barrels filled with straw along Narrow Street to the Conservative headquarters at the Angel Hotel on the corner of Priestgate and Narrow Bridge Street. Past experience meant that hotel staff and guests were ready with water to throw from upstairs windows on to the people and burning barrels below. Police and shopkeepers prepared to protect property as once again matters got out of hand. Windows were always boarded up around the Square on election nights. Thirty-five constables armed with batons charged into the crowd to clear the Square but later more than 900 people complained at police treatment. Nothing was done as it was agreed that the police themselves had been attacked first. More police were called up to deal with future election night riots.

8 June

William Bailey was landlord of the Swan Inn in Midgate; he was also a hay and straw merchant and auctioneer. In 1896 he ran a horse omnibus business with James Averill and demand for the new transport services was very great, mainly to carry people to and from the outskirts to the centre of town. The business was so successful that on June 1896 it became a limited company with Bailey as the general manager. Having started with only five vehicles and twenty-nine horses, Bailey was running twelve vehicles and fifty-four horses only a year later. He told the local newspaper that he bought the best horses to ensure a good service. People benefited because it gave those without their own transport an easy way to get to market and the town benefited from increased trade. The busiest route for the drivers was from Stanground to New England and the busiest days were Saturdays and bank holidays, though the busiest time of all was during the Peterborough Agricultural Show. There were excursions to places such as Crowland Abbey or special trips for local groups. Horse-drawn buses gave way to trams in 1903 and motor buses in 1930.

24 January

Being tall is not normally a job requirement but half of the thirty men employed to work on Peterborough's new tram system were chosen to be drivers as they were taller than the others. When the first tram left on 24 January 1903, crowds of people in Market Square had to be left behind because the turnout was so great. The local paper reported that by three in the afternoon 600 people had ridden on the trams, most of them just enjoying the novelty of the ride rather than going to a specific place. Not everyone was happy – a man collapsed with shock when he saw a tram coming, believing a railway engine had come off the tracks and was out of control. There were three routes running from eight in the morning to eleven at night every day of the week except Sunday, when there was a reduced service. Trams travelled at 12mph on the fastest section of the route and returned to their depot at Millfield, where there is a bus depot today. Extra services were laid on for workers when Peterbrotherhood opened, though some travellers had to hang on to the outside to get a ride. Trams ceased to operate in November 1930.

14 September

William Cody, known as 'Buffalo Bill', started his Wild West Show in 1882 after working as a scout for the cavalry, a Pony Express rider, a stagecoach driver and a buffalo hunter. He toured Europe and America with great success and in 1903 came to Peterborough, where he was said to be disappointed at the size of the crowd. Three train loads of people, animals and equipment arrived at the station during the night and were offloaded into wagons early next morning and taken to Padholme Road fields. Members of the public were allowed in at half-past ten in the morning of 14 September before the afternoon and evening performances. The crowds wandered round, fascinated by the cowboys and the colourful costumes of the Cossacks and Native American warriors. The show opened with a band riding into the arena playing the 'Star-Spangled Banner'. With a 'noise like thunder', the Cossacks, cowboys, tribesmen and cavalry galloped in next and lined up to await the arrival of Buffalo Bill himself, riding his pure white horse. Excited crowds were thrilled to see displays of shooting and riding but the highlight was a recreation of an attack on the Deadwood Stage. Some 14,000 people, nearly half the population, had witnessed one of the greatest entertainments of the age.

12 January

Proving that Peterborough seemed to enjoy the 'entertainment' of post-election celebrations as much, if not more, than the results themselves, 1906 was a night to remember in the town's political history. After years of dealing with riotous behaviour on election nights, increased numbers of policemen were keeping an eye on areas where tar barrels might appear. Unfortunately, they were outwitted by those determined to keep up local traditions. Those involved were undoubtedly a hooligan element, intent on causing trouble, rather than supporters of any parliamentary candidate.

George Greenwood, representing the Liberal Party, had been declared the winner and was due to leave Market Square for the Liberal Party Headquarters in Boroughbury in a hired horse-drawn cab. However, mischief-makers took away the horse whilst Greenwood was inside. Undeterred, he got in the cab and it was dragged back to his hotel by supporters. At this point, the unruly elements of the crowd took over, filling the carriage with hay and lighting it, before attempting to get it to the usual destination, the Angel Hotel. Fortunately they did not succeed – the carriage burned fiercely until all that was left was the frame! Once again the Angel Hotel (which was pulled down when W.H. Smith was built) escaped being set on fire.

24 May

Philanthropist Andrew Carnegie opened Peterborough's first public library on 24 May 1906 at a ceremony outside the building on Broadway. Having made his fortune in the American steel industry, Carnegie wanted to make education accessible to all and so he built and equipped thousands of libraries on land supplied by town councils that had to promise to maintain the library once it was built. On the day of the grand opening, Andrew Carnegie arrived at Peterborough Station, which had been specially decorated with bunting for the occasion. The mayor and other local officials and dignitaries met him there before driving to the Guildhall for a formal lunch. Afterwards, the party walked in procession to the new free library where the mayor and Mr Carnegie stood on a specially erected platform to deliver the speeches. A second platform for ladies was placed opposite in the Cattle Market area. Huge crowds had gathered and cheered loudly as they watched the opening ceremony and saw Carnegie become the first person to be awarded the Freedom of Peterborough. The certificate was in a 'handsomely carved box' made from wood that was taken from a beam in the cathedral. Nowadays, Peterborough has a new library but the original Carnegie Library building on Broadway still remains.

16 September

The Hippodrome Theatre on Broadway was a variety theatre built by a London company and it opened on 16 September 1907, giving Peterborough its second theatre – the Theatre Royal was across the road. The Hippodrome specialised in variety shows and was an extremely popular destination for Peterborough residents wanting a night out. The corrugated-iron roof caused problems for the cast and audience when it rained and when it was taken over by Fred Karno's Company a year later, the first performance had to be stopped when the noise from hailstones became too deafening. Karno was the greatest music hall impresario of the day and, thanks to his success and contacts in the world of entertainment, all the famous music hall stars of the day performed there, including Marie Lloyd and Charlie Chaplin. Over the years different owners, name changes and rebuilding meant that film shows were added to the repertoire – and could be heard when the roof was replaced! Broadway became the home of most of the cinema and variety theatres in the town but none of them seems to have had trouble attracting the crowds. The theatre was pulled down in 1937 and a Tesco supermarket now occupies the site. In 1973 the Key Theatre was opened on the Embankment alongside the River Nene.

8 November

Suffragettes marching from Edinburgh to London stopped off in Peterborough and attempted to hold a meeting at the Stanley Recreation Ground. Thousands turned up to hear their views but shortly after the speeches began some of the crowd tried to break up the meeting. They stormed the stage that had been set up and threw fireworks at the speakers. The police escorted the women to a hotel for their safety but the objectors followed and stayed outside the hotel for some time, booing and singing. Despite the violent reaction to the campaigners on this occasion, only a few months later Emmeline Pankhurst came to speak in the Corn Exchange. Banners in purple and green, colours adopted by the supporters of women's right to vote, decorated the building, along with campaign statements such as 'Keep on Pestering'. The meeting was well attended by men and women and the local newspaper wrote that Mrs Pankhurst was 'One of the most remarkable of our present-day celebrities and yet there is the acknowledgement that opinions may be bitterly opposed both to the principle and the methods of woman suffrage.' Generally votes for women did not give rise to any serious incidents in the town.

16 April

Crescent Bridge was opened on this day, to the relief of Peterborough people who had previously used a double level crossing near the old Midland Station. It was named after a crescent of Georgian houses, which unfortunately had to be demolished when the bridge was constructed. The bridge replaced a dangerous crossing that went over two lines towards Thorpe Road – operated by the Great Northern and the Midland railways. The space between them meant that people and vehicles could be trapped between two trains as they passed and there were frequent accidents and people were killed. In 1881, following the death of a young woman who was killed as she attempted to cross the second line, it was decided that a bridge would be built. A temporary subway was constructed to ease the problem until the building works were completed. As the mayor was ill, the opening ceremony was performed by his wife, Mrs J.G. Barford. A party of civic dignitaries processed along Cumbergate to Crescent Bridge and after Mrs Barford cut the blue ribbons and declared it open, they walked over the bridge and back. As the ceremony finished, workmen were already boarding up the old subway.

15 August

The year 1914 saw the rise of anti-German feeling directed at people of German origins who were living and working in this country at the outbreak of the First World War. In Peterborough, some locals took out their anger on the families of two German shopkeepers, Frank and Metz, who had run butcher's shops in the town for several years. A crowd gathered outside Frank Bros and launched a 'savage attack' on the shop and on the family home. The local yeomanry was called out to control the mob and the Riot Act was read out by the mayor, Sir Richard Wingfield. The reading of the Act gave special powers of arrest and 15 August 1914 was the last time it was used in Peterborough. Tempers had not really cooled by the following day when auctioneers arrived to dispose of the stock remaining after the rioting. As customers came out with their purchases they were themselves set upon and the food grabbed by the angry crowd. Hams were used to smash more windows and sausages thrown up in the air to hang from lampposts. About twenty people were arrested and the violent protests eventually stopped. Frank Bros continued to run a business in Peterborough despite the actions of some townspeople in 1914.

2 August

In the middle of the First World War, townspeople came together to honour a soldier who died as a result of wounds received during the Battle of the Somme. The civic funeral was not held for a local hero, however, but for Sergeant Thomas Hunter who had been serving with the Australia and New Zealand Army Corps (ANZAC) in France. He was so severely wounded that it was decided to move him to a hospital in England where he could receive specialist treatment. Unfortunately, during the long journey his condition deteriorated so much that the train stopped in Peterborough to allow him to be taken to the nearest hospital. When he died the following day, no one knew anything of his history and arrangements were made to bury him in Peterborough. In fact, he had been born in County Durham and had emigrated to Australia where he volunteered for the Australian Expeditionary Force.

His death, so far from home, aroused great sympathy in the town and crowds lined the streets for his funeral procession to the Broadway Cemetery. Thomas Hunter became known locally as the lonely ANZAC and a plaque in Peterborough Cathedral commemorates his life.

1 July

At quarter-past seven on the morning of 1 July 1928 the move to the new Memorial Hospital began. The old infirmary in Priestgate (now the museum) had been in use since 1856 when it had been established in a converted town house, owned by Earl Fitzwilliam. At the end of the First World War the 6th Northamptonshire Regiment had suggested that a purpose-built hospital would be a suitable memorial to those who had lost their lives. An appeal was launched in 1919 to raise the necessary funds but work finally began in 1925 after a Mr Bunting gave land and a house on the corner of Thorpe Road and Midland Road. The first job was to move the operating table so that it could be set up ready for use. Fifty bedridden patients then needed to be transferred from Priestgate and this was done by carrying them in their beds, two at a time, into a pantechnicon, a large vehicle normally used for transporting furniture. Nurses travelled with them as they were driven to the new hospital. Besides extra facilities such as a casualty department and convalescent ward, the new hospital more than doubled the number of patients who could be treated.

28 June

The appearance and character of the town's main street changed completely from 1929 when Narrow Bridge Street was demolished on the east side prior to the building of the Town Hall. Narrow Bridge Street led from Cathedral Square to the point where it now crosses Bourges Boulevard to join Broad Bridge Street, following the original road from the river to the abbey. The road was formerly known as Hythegate as it led to the hythes, or wharves on the river. For over 800 years it was the main road through the city, although in parts it was so narrow that two carts could not pass. Prince George, who would later become Duke of Kent, laid the foundation stone of the Town Hall on 28 June 1929. An old newsreel film shows his car making its way with difficulty down Narrow Bridge Street. Crowds lined the road and leant from windows to cheer him on his way and it is clear that there was only just enough room to let the procession pass. The bustling shops and businesses that once lined the road disappeared to be replaced by the Town Hall in 1933 and the old Narrow Bridge Street passed into history.

7 June

Following on from earlier engineering work that had developed in Peterborough, June 1932 saw the establishment of a firm that was to become the city's biggest employer. W.P. Stanley had started a small iron foundry on Queen Street in the centre of Peterborough, where the Queensgate Shopping Centre stands today. The site, which also repaired and made some agricultural machinery, was taken over by Barford and Thomas Perkins, who produced road rollers. Thomas Perkins' grandson, Francis (Frank) Perkins set up his own company in 1932 with Charles Chapman and they began to develop and manufacture high-speed, lightweight, diesel engines. From the small Queen Street factory with only seven workers, Frank Perkins Limited went on to worldwide success and by the 1950s the firm employed 7,000 people. The new works were opened in 1947 and above the entrance Frank Perkins put his personal motto – 'Where there is no vision, the people perish', which is a quote from the Bible. In 1959 the company was bought by tractor manufacturers Massey Ferguson, who had been their biggest customers. In 1998, the firm became part of the Caterpillar Group. Along with other firms such as Baker Perkins and Peterbrotherhood, Perkins made Peterborough a major engineering town. Henry Royce of Rolls-Royce fame was born in Alwalton and trained in Peterborough.

26 October

Peterborough's new Town Hall was opened by Alderman Whitsed on Bridge Street on this date. The first meeting hall to be used for town business after the Reformation was erected in about 1572 by the Feoffees and was probably a single-storey building where butter was sold – records show rents being paid by butter sellers in 1614. In 1671 the present Guildhall, 'a chamber over the cross', was built for public meetings, magistrates' courts, copyhold courts and parliamentary elections. In 1874 it was handed over to the Corporation to be used as a Town Hall. Alterations made two years later were not welcomed by everyone as oak panels were removed and coloured glass replaced by plain glass. The Guildhall was not big enough for the council's use and in 1901 an extension was built to include the Mayor's Parlour and Town Clerk's office. By 1926 a report on the deterioration of the building was commissioned to see what work needed doing to make it safe. Peterborough Improvement Act 1927 authorised a new Town Hall in Narrow Bridge Street but decided that the old Guildhall should be preserved as it was an important ancient building, of which there were few in Peterborough apart from the cathedral.

28 May

The Mayor of Peterborough unveiled the open-air swimming pool in May 1936 and it is still a popular leisure facility in the city today. The art deco-style building stands in landscaped grounds near the Embankment and has been regularly renovated. The first pool was not heated, but that did not deter the thousands who crowded into Peterborough Lido during the summer months. There were springboards and a diving board and in the early years there was also a water chute. Early visitors remember buying cups of Oxo and slices of jam and bread, no doubt welcome when they wanted to warm up on chillier days. In the 1930s people had more time and money to spend on healthy exercise and leisure activities than before and days out at the Lido provided both. The first bomb to fall on Peterborough in the Second World War landed on the corner of the Lido. At one time there were plans to knock it down but now it is a listed building and is still as popular today. There are now three heated pools, one of which is 50m long, providing the city with its only Olympic-length swimming pool.

10 August

Considering the major engineering works, railway sheds and airfields around the city, Peterborough did not suffer as many air raids as might have been expected. On the night of 9–10 August 1942, however, over 200 incendiary bombs landed on buildings in the town centre, including the cathedral, Town Hall and several business premises. ARP (Air Raid Precautions) wardens and Fire Watchers acted to prevent fires spreading through the town centre. Six firebombs landed on the cathedral itself and another thirty on the Town Hall, but thanks to the quick thinking of the Fire Watchers, no damage was done. The Fire Watchers' Memorial in the cathedral commemorates those who protected the building during the Second World War: 'Remember the Fire Watchers led by SOG Wilson who guarded these roofs in time of war. They twice saved the cathedral from firebombs 1941–44.' Most of the incendiary devices fell in the Bridge Street area and although roof fires started in a number of buildings, they were quickly dealt with. At the City Cinema, which stood on the site now occupied by the Marks & Spencer store, the stage and organ were badly damaged and the cinema was out of action for several weeks.

21 March

Winds gusting at over 90mph swept through the town on this day, damaging property and uprooting trees. A number of people were killed or injured by the falling debris. The upper portion of one of the cathedral pinnacles was blown off and a 5ft-long block of masonry fell into the graveyard below. A telegraph pole blocked the railway line at New England and steel scaffolding crashed through the roof at Westwood Works. The 500ft corrugated-iron roof blew off the engine shop at Brotherhoods and a 60ft chimney collapsed at the iron foundry. On the same day the North Level barrier bank at Crowland was breached by water, which surged across the Fens. Over 12,000 acres of Fenland was flooded and livestock was swept away. Stone sent to breach the gap could not get through quickly enough so nearly a mile of light railway lines were laid to carry it to where it was needed. Villagers, cadets and German prisoners worked day and night, and finally the breach was blocked with sixteen amphibious 'water buffalo' tanks. Thousands of tons of potatoes were lost but the RSPCA managed to rescue stranded animals.

22 August

Even today the centre of Peterborough is small and shops line street patterns that have been there for hundreds of years. Cowgate is one of the oldest roads in the town and it was nearly destroyed in a blaze that began in the Robert Sayles' building on 22 August 1956. The fire was spotted in the early evening but within two hours had turned into an inferno that completely destroyed Peterborough's largest store, along with other shops along Cowgate. The Volunteer Fire Brigade were on the scene but their engines were nearly destroyed as the fire took hold. Over 100 firemen, two of whom were injured, fought the blaze, including an American fire crew from RAF Alconbury. As flames rose over 100ft into the air, firemen had to pump water from the River Nene to put out the fire. The incident emphasised the need for more water hydrants in the town to provide a quicker supply in an emergency. Robert Sayles' four-storey building was completely gutted and the company decided that they could not salvage anything from the ruins. Despite the intensity of the blaze and the flames that spread across the street, no one lost their lives and only one family was made homeless.

25 May

Peterborough United Football Club came into existence at a meeting at the Angel Hotel in 1934, replacing the old Peterborough and Fletton United that had ceased to exist two years earlier. One of the most important events in Peterborough United's history was the team's admission into the Football League on 25 May 1960. At that time there was no automatic promotion from the lower levels of football to the old Fourth Division, instead clubs with the most votes were selected whether or not they had won their local group. Despite being champions of their Midlands League six times, including the five seasons prior to their admission, Peterborough had never received enough votes. Finally in 1960, the club received the necessary support to allow them to move up into Division Four. Crowds surrounded the windows of the *Evening Telegraph*'s office where news of the election was posted. The town celebrated after years of disappointment. Players and officials and their wives were even invited to a free night out courtesy of Chipperfield's Circus, which was visiting the town in June. The club's nickname 'Posh' probably came about when player/manager Pat Tirrel said in 1921 that the club needed 'posh players for a posh team'.

17 March

On 17 March 1963, with their single 'Love Me Do' at number seventeen in the charts, The Beatles returned to the Embassy Theatre (now Edwards) as a supporting act to Tommy Roe and Chris Montez. The reaction of the audience was entirely different to the first time they had appeared, on 2 December the previous year, at which event local reporter Lyndon Whittaker had written that, 'the exciting Beatles rock group quite frankly failed to excite me. The drummer apparently thought his job was to lead, not to provide rhythm. He made far too much noise and in their final number "Twist and Shout" it sounded as if everyone was trying to make more noise than the others. In a more mellow mood their "A Taste of Honey" was much better and "Love Me Do" was tolerable.' The audience had booed and yelled 'Get off!' and 'Rubbish!'. Manager Brian Epstein had arranged their appearance with a local promoter who booked them to appear in a Frank Ifield show. The group received no payment for this performance, only their travel expenses. This time their performance in Peterborough left the audience screaming for more. Following their earlier reception it was perhaps surprising that they had been invited back but it was not long before their records began to top the charts and 'Beatlemania' began.

27 July

When Peterborough was granted New Town status in July 1967, plans were made for four townships surrounding the city. Although easy access to and from the new suburbs was guaranteed by a new road network, each township was built round its own district centre. Shops, schools, health centres, parks, leisure and sporting facilities and community centres were built at the same time as residential accommodation. The first of the townships was Bretton, where construction of 5,000 houses began at the beginning of the 1970s. Pedestrian and cycle paths and cul-de-sacs were designed to keep heavy traffic away from residential areas, which were landscaped and surrounded by existing woodland and farmland. The first residents moved to Bretton in 1972 and benefited from a central district heating system. Having been designed to accommodate families moving from areas of high population like London, jobs were created by companies like Thomas Cook, who took advantage of the benefits of moving their new head offices into the township. Since then, new townships at Orton, Werrington and Hampton have been built. Once more the population of Peterborough has increased dramatically in a short period of time and the boundaries of the city have expanded even further.

27 March

Peterborough welcomed the Queen and Prince Philip when the Royal Maundy service was held in the cathedral. The town had been decorated with flags and banners and work on the pedestrianisation of Bridge Street had just been completed in time for a royal walkabout. The Town Hall and the station had been given a new coat of paint and shrubs and trees had been planted. Forty-nine women and forty-nine men, reflecting the Queen's age at the time, were chosen to receive the leather purses containing the specially minted Maundy money. The tradition of monarchs giving coins, clothes and food to the needy and elderly has changed through the years but the ceremony is still a colourful affair. Yeomen of the Guard accompanied the Queen into the cathedral for the short service before the royal party made their way to the Town Hall for lunch. As she left to walk through the Precincts, the Queen was shown a new statue of herself by Alan Durst, in the left-hand arch of the West Front. Walkabouts were quite a new idea then and the crowds lining the route were able to get close to the Queen and Prince Philip, making it a memorable day for the city.

10 September

Articles found in a newly ploughed field at Water Newton in February 1975 were declared a treasure trove (buried with the hope of later discovery) on 10 September. The objects were discovered in the area of the Roman town of Durobrivae and confirmed the wealth and status of inhabitants in the centuries after the first Roman settlement. Romans of the Ninth Legion first came to the area in AD 45 and built a fort at what is now Longthorpe. Its position near the Nene on the Fen Edge made it a good base for controlling the Britons in the east of the country and roads were built which, in combination with river transport, ensured excellent communications. A settlement initially serving the fort grew up along the Nene and Durobrivae – 'the fort by the bridge' – continued to grow into a town right at the point where Ermine Street crossed the river. A large pottery industry developed producing 'Castorware', which was found throughout Britain and abroad.

The objects found in 1975 date from the fourth century and are the earliest known examples of silverware for use in the Christian Church. Most of the small plaques were probably offerings given by members of a local Christian community.

4 June

Reverend Pattern purchased a steam engine in 1968 but it took years of hard work and preparation before the Nene Valley Railway ran its first services in June 1977. The trains originally ran from Wansford to Orton Mere but the line has been extended from Yarwell to the Nene Valley Station in Peterborough. The 7.5-mile track follows part of Peterborough's first train route, the mid-nineteenth-century London to Birmingham railway. Passengers can enjoy views of Ferry Meadows Country Park and the River Nene as they travel to the city centre.

The Nene Valley Railway is unique in having engines and carriages from several different countries and this has made it popular with film-makers. It has provided locations for films such as *Octopussy* and *Goldeneye*, television programmes including *Poirot*, *Eastenders* and *Secret Army* and a music video by Queen. Volunteers have made the railway one of the top attractions in Peterborough, recalling the city's long railway history and engineering heritage. Its popularity today is in marked contrast to the opposition from local landowners when the line was first proposed. The *Railway Times* commented on Earl Fitzwilliam's initial opposition to the railway crossing his land, whilst agreeing that it could cross other people's property.

1 July

One of Peterborough's most popular amenities is Ferry Meadows Country Park, which opened on this date in 1978. It forms part of Nene Park, which runs from the city centre along the River Nene as far as Wansford. The whole area of agricultural land was unsuitable for building development as it ran alongside the flood plain of the Nene. Therefore, when New Town status was granted to Peterborough, the idea of a country park was born. Gravel for building new roads was taken from the site and created the three lakes that are central to Ferry Meadows. Work on the site also revealed evidence of early occupation in the area that dated back 5,000 years and included a Roman farm. Sailing, walking, cycling, horse riding, fishing and wildlife are just some of the attractions of the park, which covers over 500 acres. The Nene Valley Railway runs along the edge of Ferry Meadows and there is a railway station at the entrance. The area takes its name from Milton Ferry Bridge, which crosses the Nene into the park. The ferry toll gates were opened on payment of a small fee until the early 1960s. Until recently, the park was the location for the annual Firework Fiesta.

9 March

The biggest change to the centre of Peterborough since the twelfth century was the building of the Queensgate Shopping Centre, which covers the area once occupied by the medieval town centre. Queensgate opened for business on 9 March 1982, but was formally opened on 18 November of that year by Queen Beatrix of the Netherlands. When Peterborough achieved New Town status it was decided that the city needed a modern shopping complex, incorporating car parking and a new bus station. A walkway links the shopping centre to the railway station, giving easy access for shoppers coming from outside the city. The development meant that some of the old streets that had formed the centre of Peterborough since the Middle Ages disappeared under the new building. Queen Street had been the site of the General Post Office and the first Barford and Perkins ironworks. Narrow streets like Cumbergate had been at the industrial heart of the town since the twelfth century, housing workers in the wool and leather trades. The path through Queensgate follows part of the old street pattern. The new shopping centre encouraged many large companies to open stores in the city and provided increased employment locally.

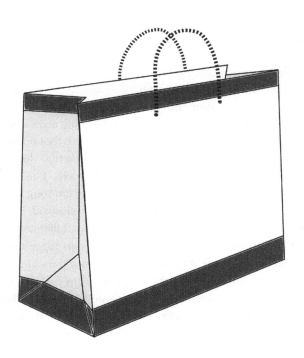

3 November

In November 1982, archaeologist Dr Francis Prior literally stumbled on the site that is now recognised as one of the most important Bronze Age sites in Europe. Having spent many years investigating and recording the Fengate area of Peterborough before the site was developed, Dr Prior had found evidence of early settlements dating from the Bronze Age. After recording part of the Fen Causeway, a Roman road leading across the area, he was walking along a dyke when he caught his foot on the end of a wooden post. He immediately recognised that the end of the post had been shaped by a Bronze Age axe. The find led him to eventually uncover the remains of a 1km-long wooden causeway across the Fen, leading to an artificial island. The line of posts followed an earlier way that was about 2,000 years older. Many objects were found around the taller posts suggesting that they were deliberately thrown as offerings into the water. Some of the hundreds of metal objects came from Europe, whilst jewellery and flour-grinding stones came from across Britain. The recent discovery of eight beautifully preserved Bronze Age log boats emphasizes Flag Fen's position as one of Europe's most important archaeological sites.

1 April

In 1998 Peterborough was made a unitary authority, separate from the county of Cambridgeshire. The central area of the new authority is similar to the area of the ancient Soke. Nowadays it extends to the west past Burghley House to Wothorpe, to the east as far as Thorney Toll, south to Norman Cross and north beyond Deeping Gate. The Soke of Peterborough as an administrative district was geographically part of Northamptonshire until the county of Huntingdon and Peterborough was created, only to disappear in 1972 into Cambridgeshire. Until the arrival of railways and the growth of the engineering industry, Peterborough was a relatively small market town with administrative authority over the Soke. The ancient Soke was under the control of Peterborough's abbey and encompassed countryside, woods, fenland and villages, which gradually became part of the growing city. The town and rural areas combined to keep Peterborough a place where agriculture was, and is, an important part of the local economy. Despite the spread of business and housing developments around the town in the form of new 'townships' with their own local centres, the historic heart of Peterborough still covers a relatively small area and the street pattern remains much as it has been for centuries.

3 September

Peterborough's Green Wheel Cycle Route forms a 50-mile (80km) circular path around the city and the 'spokes' of the Green Wheel converge on the town centre. Peterborough has always had extensive cycle paths, especially in the new townships, and the creation of the Green Wheel was a Millennium project to link routes around surrounding villages and countryside. The Green Wheel also connects to the National Cycle Network. In 1993 Peterborough was designated one of the United Kingdom's four environment cities and, as part of on-going policy, the aim was to improve 'green' travel between residential areas and the city centre or places of work. Following the Green Wheel's entire circular route takes cyclists around places of interest such as country parks, villages and historical sites including the Flag Fen Bronze Age Centre. There are information boards that help locals and tourists learn more about the landscape through which they are travelling, as well as features such as sculptures and the Shanks Millennium Bridge. Passing through the city, residential areas, fenland and stone-built villages, the Green Wheel reflects Peterborough's industrial and agricultural heritage, dating back to prehistoric times. The development of cycle-friendly routes is a continuing process that provides more leisure opportunities as well as a 'greener' city.

22 November

Early in the evening of 22 November 2001, the cathedral verger noticed a glowing light shining from inside the church as he was walking through the Minster Precincts. A small votive candle had been left on a pile of plastic chairs which, although slow to light initially, melted to cause a fierce blaze. Fire threatened to destroy the building but fortunately the fire brigade was able to tackle the flames before they reached the wooden ceiling, dating from the twelfth century. The following day revealed the enormous task that awaited those who had to clean and repair the damage to the building. The whole interior was covered in thick black soot, some window glass was broken (fortunately not a stained-glass window) and the organ had to be dismantled for cleaning after a screen behind it was badly damaged. Ironically, cleaning of the painted nave ceiling had almost been completed when the fire happened, so work had to start again. As the work of cleaning the stonework went on, early wall paintings were revealed for the first time in hundreds of years. Following the fire, the cathedral remained open for worship and continues to be one of the glories of Peterborough.

20 January

Today's *Evening Telegraph* reported that the name of a riverside footpath would not be changed to Walter's Leap in honour of local personality Walter Cornelius. A former circus strongman who as a youngster had come from Latvia to England, Walter was a swimming pool attendant at Peterborough Lido. He was much loved in Peterborough for his work for charity and for his daredevil stunts, including having concrete slabs broken on his head, skipping with an 8ft steel rope, pushing a double-decker bus with his head for half a mile and pushing a pea up a hill with his nose. However, it was as Peterborough's 'birdman' that he drew the crowds as he attempted to fly across the River Nene using homemade wings. Launching himself from the top of a local supermarket, which was next to the water by the Town Bridge, he would inevitably plummet straight down into the water, raising loud cheers from the spectators. In 1972, following another failed attempt to fly across the Nene, he said, 'It was a bit painful but I still think I can fly. Next time I shall have to wear stronger elastic, and I think the wings were too flimsy. Unfortunately I was in the water before I was able to start flapping my arms.'

4 March

The formal opening of the £10 million University Centre Peterborough (UCP) facility for higher education on Park Crescent came after years of planning. Educational facilities in Peterborough had steadily advanced over the course of the twentieth century and into the twenty-first. In 1903 a technical college (now the College Arms) opened on Broadway to train apprentices for the local engineering industry and offered courses such as science, maths and technical drawing for boys and commercial subjects for girls. The demand for apprentices grew so much that the Peterborough Technical College (later the Regional College) followed it, opening in 1952. By the 1990s Loughborough University was offering courses but sadly this service ended in 2003. However, a few diplomas and degrees awarded by Anglia Ruskin University were being offered at the Peterborough Regional College and in 2007 a formal agreement was reached between these two institutions to work together to further higher education in the city. The University Centre was developed from this scheme and is located in the grounds of the Regional College. It is hoped that the UCP will provide a good basis for building up access to higher degrees and improving the quality of education available locally. Over the next ten years the campus and courses will be extended, encouraging more people to study in the city.

9 July

A service took place in the city centre on this day to rebury the remains of Peterborough citizens who had died at least 500 years ago. Workmen uncovered the previously unknown burial site while they were landscaping the area around the parish church of St John's in Cathedral Square. St John's replaced Peterborough's first parish church, which was in the old Saxon quarter, now the Boongate area. It was rebuilt in the market place in the fifteenth century, using stone from the old church and from the front of the Becket Chapel on the left of the cathedral gates. Unlike other town cemeteries, there was no record of a graveyard and it has always been assumed that there was no churchyard in the middle of town.

The burials were laid out in lines facing east, as is usual in Christian graveyards. One person, thought to be a priest, faces the other way towards his parishioners. Despite the lack of any mention of the cemetery, the history of the town centre must now be reconsidered. Landscaping work was moved so as not to disturb any more graves, which were obviously in the same area. A memorial plaque commemorates those who were laid to rest at St John's.

17 December

At the end of 2014 plans were announced to change the face of part of Peterborough city centre in the Westgate area, next to the Queensgate Shopping Centre and across from the railway station. Westgate took its name from the websters or wool weavers who worked on this road or *gata* in medieval times. Later the road was the main route through Peterborough for stagecoaches and there is still an old milestone that shows the distance to London after driving down Westgate. Following the construction of Bourges Boulevard along the line of the railway tracks, and the building of Queensgate in the 1980s, car and coach parks took over much of the open land. The latest plans will revitalise Westgate, whilst leaving buildings like the Westgate church and the Brewery Tap pub, with its microbrewery, still standing. There will be a new hotel, multi-screen cinema, shops, restaurants, an indoor market and housing. Until late in the nineteenth century, Westgate marked the edge of Peterborough's small historic town centre. From 2015 and into the future, hopefully all of Westgate will become once again a busy and popular part of Peterborough life.

Bibliography

Mellows, Charles and William Thomas (translated and edited),
   The Peterborough Chronicle of Hugh Candidus (1941)
Pryor, Francis, *Flag Fen: Life and Death of a Prehistoric Landscape*
   (The History Press, 2005)
Tebbs, H.F., *Peterborough: A History* (The Oleander Press, 1979)
The CAMUS Project, *Five Parishes Their People and Their Places*
   (2004)
Walker, T.J., *The Depot for Prisoners of War at Norman Cross,
   Huntingdonshire, 1796 to 1816* (1913)

Other source material provided courtesy of:
Northants Record Office
Peterborough Cathedral
Peterborough Local Studies and Archives Central Library

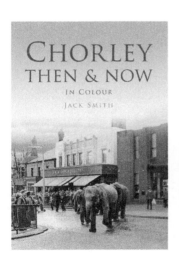
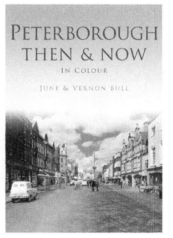

Lightning Source UK Ltd.
Milton Keynes UK
UKOW06f1136290515

252537UK00001B/1/P

9 780750 961530